THE FOX BOOK

THE
FOX BOOK

compiled and edited by

RICHARD SHAW

Illustrated

FREDERICK WARNE AND COMPANY, INC.
New York and London

ACKNOWLEDGEMENTS

The editor and publishers wish to thank the following for their kind permission to reproduce copyrighted material used in this anthology. The publishers have made every effort to locate the owners of material used. If any omissions have been made, they offer their sincere apologies. Such omissions will be corrected in subsequent editions provided notification is sent to the publishers.

P. 24 "Four Little Foxes" from COVENANT WITH EARTH by Lew Sarett. Edited and copyrighted, 1956, by Alma Johnson Sarett, and published 1956, by the University of Florida Press. Reprinted by permission of Mrs. Sarett. P. 40 "Little Fox Lost" from THE LITTLE WHISTLER by Frances Frost. Copyright 1949 by McGraw-Hill, Inc. Used with permission of McGraw-Hill Book Company. P. 41 "Night of Wind" from POOL IN THE MEADOW by Frances Frost, published by the Houghton Mifflin Company and used with their permission. P. 42 "The Spun Gold Fox," Copyright © 1963 by Patricia Hubbell. From THE APPLE VENDOR'S FAIR. Used by permission of Atheneum Publishers. P. 47 "The Fox and the Chickens" is reprinted with the permission of Charles Scribner's Sons from THE THREE SPARROWS by Christian Morgenstern, translated by Max Knight. Translation copyright © 1968 Max Knight.

ISBN 0 7232 6082 6

Everyone knows foxes are clever. But not everyone knows just how clever. Old foxes are hard to fool and almost impossible to catch for they learn quickly and they remember things. To escape pursuing hounds, foxes will cover their trails by wading in streams, walking the tops of rail fences and riding on the backs of sheep. But of the four kinds of foxes—red, gray, actic and kit—only the gray fox climbs trees.

Fox stories are told all over the world. In some the fox changes into a beautiful woman. In others he brings Easter eggs before dawn. And in at least one he sports nine beautiful tails. But no matter how he looks or what he does, the fox is always clever. Sometimes too clever.

THE ARTISTS WHO CREATED
THE ILLUSTRATIONS ARE:

The illustrations are on
the following pages:

"For Karen"

SLY IS THE WORD

Some people are busy—
As busy as bees—
And others are quiet as mice;
Or eager as beavers,
Or crazy as loons,
Or happy as larks—which is nice.
Some people are stubborn—
As stubborn as mules—
And others are dumb as an ox;
But never was anyone,
Anywhere, anytime
Nearly as sly as a fox.

—*Richard Shaw*

THE RAVEN AND THE FOX

High on the branch of a great oak tree sat a jet black Raven. He was croaking with joy for he had just found at the foot of the tree a piece of savory meat. He croaked to tell the world of his good luck, not knowing that the meat had been poisoned and put there by a farmer whose chickens were being stolen by a Fox. The farmer hoped the greedy Fox would gulp down the meat and meet a well deserved death.

The Fox heard the Raven's croaking and, from the ground below, called, "Ah, there you are, Royal Eagle!"

The Raven glanced down at the Fox and asked, "What did you say?"

"I wondered," replied the Fox, "if you were the Royal Eagle whom the Gods send to this oak every day to feed me, for I see you have a piece of savory meat in your sharp talons."

The Raven was not only astonished, he was delighted at being mistaken for the Royal Eagle, just as the Fox knew he would be. And, just as the Fox had planned, the stupid Raven let the savory meat fall to the earth at the Fox's feet.

As he proudly spread his stubby wings, the Raven

croaked, "I must get back to my soaring high above the clouds with the other eagles."

And he flew away.

Laughing at the success of his trick, the Fox pounced on the meat and gulped it down.

He was dead within half an hour.

Moral: *The little lies of the flatterer may poison the flatterer too.*

—Lessing

THE WILD SILVER FOX

Down among the parsley,
Out beyond the phlox,
I have a secret place to meet
A wild silver fox.

So early on a summer's day,
When all *their* eyes are sealed,
I slip from bed without a noise
And pausing by the field,

I repeat some magic words
Like *bud* and *dawn* and *dew*,
To spellbind my excitement
Into coming true—

And then I go along the paths
Where moss conceals the rocks,
Through buttercups and bluebells
Calling "Fox?" and "Fox?"

I stop and count the graceful wheat,
Unhurried as the air,
When like a second waking up—
The sudden fox is there.

His look is very serious,
And yet his eyes are sweet,
The kind of look you look for
In the people that you meet;

And when we sit a formal time,
He half expresses smiles
That people who don't know him
Call his "crafty wiles".

And sometimes, then, he leads me
Deep among the trees;
He lets me hear the language
A fox will speak to bees.

He shows me where the rabbits go,
The bubbly haunt of frogs,
The copse of firs that hides his lair
Under fallen logs;

He knows all tiny pathways
And every hidden place
Where, whiskery and softly furred,
Each creature leaves his trace.

He counsels me in ferns and brooks
And where the minnow lies,
In mushroom dells like palaces,
And routes where pheasants rise.

Then, as the sun gets stronger—
The morning almost here—
The fox will double on our tracks
And softly as the deer,

Lead me to the other world,
And when we're at its edge,
He disappears, as foxes do,
When out beyond the hedge—

I find the phlox has opened,
The parsley green and deep,
And the swallows making music
To wake the day from sleep.

And then I go inside the house
And, putting on both socks,
I whisper to my wide-eyed toys
Of wonder and a fox.

—*Joan Hutton*

THE TRAVELS OF A FOX

One day a fox was digging behind a stump and he found a bumblebee; and the fox put the bumblebee in a bag and took the bag over his shoulder and travelled.

At the first house he came to, he went in and said to the mistress of the house, "Can I leave my bag here while I go to Squintum's?"

"Yes," said the woman.

"Then be careful not to open the bag," said the fox.

But as soon as he was out of sight the woman said to herself, "Well, I wonder what the fellow has in his bag that he is so careful about. I will look and see. It can't do any harm, for I shall tie the bag right up again."

However, the moment she unloosed the string, out flew the bumblebee, and the rooster caught him and ate him all up.

After a while the fox came back. He took up his bag and knew at once that his bumblebee was gone, and he said to the woman, "Where is my bumblebee?"

And the woman said, "I untied the string just to take a little peep to find out what was in your bag, and the bumblebee flew out and the rooster ate him."

"Very well," said the fox; "I must have the rooster, then."

So he caught the rooster and put him in his bag and travelled.

At the next house he came to, he went in and said to the mistress of the house, "Can I leave my bag here while I go to Squintum's?"

"Yes," said the woman.

"Then be careful not to open the bag," said the fox.

But as soon as he was out of sight the woman said to herself, "Well, I wonder what the fellow has in his bag that he is so careful about. I will look and see. It can't do any harm, for I shall tie the bag right up again."

However, the moment she unloosed the string the rooster flew out and the pig caught him and ate him all up.

After a while the fox came back. He took up his bag and knew at once that his rooster was gone, and he said to the woman, "Where is my rooster?"

And the woman said, "I untied the string just to take a little peep to find out what was in your bag, and the rooster flew out and the pig ate him."

"Very well," said the fox, "I must have the pig, then."

So he caught the pig and put him in his bag and travelled.

At the next house he came to, he went in and said to the mistress of the house, "Can I leave my bag here while I go to Squintum's?"

"Yes," said the woman.

"Then be careful not to open the bag," said the fox.

But as soon as he was out of sight the woman said to

herself, "Well, I wonder what the fellow has in his bag that he is so careful about. I will look and see. It can't do any harm, for I shall tie the bag right up again."

However, the moment she unloosed the string, the pig jumped out and the ox gored him.

After a while the fox came back. He took up his bag and knew at once that his pig was gone, and he said to the woman, "Where is my pig?"

And the woman said, "I untied the string just to take a little peep to find out what was in your bag, and the pig jumped out and the ox gored him."

"Very well," said the fox, "I must have the ox, then."

So he caught the ox and put him in his bag and travelled.

At the next house he came to, he went in and said to the mistress of the house, "Can I leave my bag here while I go to Squintum's?"

"Yes," said the woman.

"Then be careful not to open the bag," said the fox.

But as soon as he was out of sight the woman said to herself, "Well, I wonder what the fellow has in his bag that he is so careful about. I will look and see. It can't do any harm, for I shall tie the bag right up again."

However, the moment she unloosed the string, the ox got out, and the woman's little boy chased the ox out of the house and across a meadow and over a hill, clear out of sight.

After a while the fox came back. He took up his bag and knew at once that his ox was gone, and he said to the woman, "Where is my ox?"

And the woman said, "I untied the string just to take a little peep to find out what was in your bag, and the ox got out and my little boy chased him out of the house and across a meadow and over a hill, clear out of sight."

"Very well," said the fox, "I must have the little boy, then."

So he caught the little boy and put him in his bag and travelled.

At the next house he came to, he went in and said to the mistress of the house, "Can I leave my bag here while I go to Squintum's?"

"Yes," said the woman.

"Then be careful not to open the bag," said the fox.

The woman had been making cake, and when it was baked she took it from the oven, and her children gathered around her teasing for some of it.

"Oh, ma, give me a piece!" said one, and "Oh, ma, give me a piece!" said each of the others.

And the smell of the cake came to the little boy in the bag, and he heard the children beg for the cake, and he said, "Oh, mammy, give me a piece!"

Then the woman opened the bag and took the little boy out; and she put the house-dog in the bag in the little boy's place, and the little boy joined the other children.

After a while the fox came back. He took up his bag and he saw that it was tied fast and he thought that the little boy was safe inside. "I have been all day on the road," said he, "without a thing to eat, and I am getting hungry. I will just step off into the woods now and see how this little boy I have in my bag tastes."

So he put the bag on his back and travelled deep into the woods. Then he sat down and untied the bag, and if the little boy had been in there things would have gone badly with him.

But the little boy was at the house of the woman who made the cake, and when the fox untied the bag the house-dog jumped out and killed him.

FOUR LITTLE FOXES

Speak gently, Spring, and make no sudden sound;
For in my windy valley, yesterday I found
New-born foxes squirming on the ground—
       Speak gently.

Walk softly, March, forbear the bitter blow;
Her feet within a trap, her blood upon the snow,
The four little foxes saw their mother go—
       Walk softly.

Go lightly, Spring, oh, give them no alarm;
When I covered them with boughs to shelter
    them from harm,
The thin blue foxes suckled at my arm—
       Go lightly.

Step softly, March, with your rampant hurricane;
Nuzzling one another, and whimpering with
    pain,
The new little foxes are shivering in the rain—
       Step softly.

—Lew Sarett

25

THE FOX AND THE COCK

There once was a fox,
A sly, cunning sinner,
Who stole what he ate
For his breakfast and dinner.
"How I drool," muttered Fox,
"How my appetite quickens
At sight of those fat,
Tender, juicy, spring chickens."
But on top of the henhouse,
His eyes flashing wide,
Perched a rooster—his feathers
Aglitter with pride.
Cock's job was to crow,
And sound the alarm,
To warn against foxes
And save hens from harm.
Thought sly Fox, "If for lunch
I'm to catch a fat chick,
My brain must invent
A quick, clever trick.
I'll have to out-smart
That clever young cock
Who sits on the henhouse
While guarding his flock."

So "Amigo!" cried Fox,
"I hope you'll excuse
My just dropping by,
But I bring you good news.
All animals now
Are at peace with each other.
So you call me 'cousin,'
And I'll call you 'brother.'
Now you and your chickens
Can go for long walks,
Without fearing foxes,
Or weasels or hawks."
"Indeed!" Cock observed,
"How jolly! How grand!"
"Amigo," smiled Fox,
"Do come down—here's my hand."
"In a minute!" Cock winked.
"But I'll tarry until
Our brothers the hounds
Reach this side of the hill.
Hear their brotherly barking?—"
"They're headed this way?"
Fox exclaimed in a panic,
"I really can't stay!"
To the dark woods Fox scampered,
Aquiver with fright,

To hide from the hounds,
His eyes beady bright.
"You saved us, dear Cock,"
Clucked the hens. "You're a hero.
Without your quick thinking,
We now would be zero."
Chuckled Cock, "A real hero
Can't be chicken-hearted;
He must out-fox foxes
Or he'll be out-smarted."

          —Kay McKemy (after La Fontaine)

THE FOX

A fox jumped up one winter's night,
And begged the moon to give him light,
For he'd many miles to trot that night
Before he reached his den O!
    Den O! Den O!

For he'd many miles to trot that night
Before he reached his den O!

The first place he came to was a farmer's yard,
Where the ducks and the geese declared it hard
That their nerves should be shaken and their rest
    so marred
By a visit from Mr. Fox O!
    Fox O! Fox O!

That their nerves should be shaken and their rest
    so marred
By a visit from Mr. Fox O!

He took the grey goose by the neck,
And swung him right across his back;
The grey goose cried out, Quack, quack, quack,
With his legs hanging dangling down O!
    Down O! Down O!

The grey goose cried out, Quack, quack, quack,
With his legs hanging dangling down O!

Old Mother Slipper Slopper jumped out of bed,
And out of the window she popped her head:
Oh! John, John, John, the grey goose is gone,
And the fox is off to his den O!
    Den O! Den O!

Oh! John, John, John, the grey goose is gone,
And the fox is off to his den O!

John ran up to the top of the hill,
And blew his whistle loud and shrill;
Said the fox, That is very pretty music; still—
I'd rather be in my den O!
    Den O! Den O!

Said the fox, That is very pretty music; still—
I'd rather be in my den O!

The fox went back to his hungry den,
And his dear little foxes, eight, nine, ten;
Quoth they, Good daddy, you must go there again,
If you bring such good cheer from the farm O!
    Farm O! Farm O!

Quoth they, Good daddy, you must go there again,
If you bring such good cheer from the farm O!

The fox and his wife, without any strife,
Said they never ate a better goose in all their life:
They did very well without fork or knife,
And the little ones picked the bones O!
    Bones O! Bones O!

They did very well without fork or knife,
And the little ones picked the bones O!

THE FOX AND THE CROW

One bright day, as a Fox padded along the edge of a wood, he sniffed a most delicious smell. Following his nose, he soon found out that the smell came from a tall maple tree, or rather from a piece of cheese in a tall maple tree, or rather from a piece of cheese in the beak of a Crow perched high on a branch of a tall maple tree.

Like all foxes, this Fox had a very good appetite— especially for spicy cheese.

"How can I make the crow open his beak and drop the cheese down to me?" the Fox wondered to himself.

After a moment's thought, he called to the Crow, "Crow, how do you keep your feathers so shiny and black?"

But the Crow didn't answer.

"Crow," called the Fox a second time, "how is it that you have such a beautiful shape?"

Still the Crow didn't answer.

Then the Fox called, "Crow, it certainly is a shame that your voice is not so beautiful as your shiny feathers and your beautiful shape; for if it were, you would certainly be called the Queen of Birds, and rightly so."

The foolish Crow, who believed that she sang the most beautiful of songs and wanted so very much to be

the Queen of Birds, then opened her beak and croaked,
"Caw! Caw! Caw-Caw!"

And the cheese dropped into the Fox's waiting mouth.

"Thank you, Queen of Birds," called the Fox, "you sing almost as well as you think."

—Aesop

THE TWO FOXES

On a winter's night
When the moon shone bright,
Two foxes went out for their prey;
As they trotted along
With frolic and song
They cheered the lonely way.

Through the woods they went
But they could not scent
A rabbit or goose astray,
Till at length they came
To some better game
In a farmer's barn by the way.

On the roost, there sat
Some chickens as fat
As foxes could wish for their dinners
So the prowlers found
A hole in the ground
And both went in, the sinners!

They both went in
With a squeeze and a grin;
And the chickens were quickly killed
And one of them munched
And feasted and lunched,
Till his stomach was fairly filled.

The other, more wise,
Looked about with both eyes
And scarcely did eat at all;
For as he came in
With a squeeze and a grin
He remarked that the hole was small.

Thus matters went on
Till the night was gone,
And the farmer came out with a pole.
Both foxes flew,
And one got through,
But the greedy one stuck in the hole.

So full was his pluck,
Of the chickens he had been eating.
He could neither get out
Nor turn about,
And so he was killed by beating.

And thus, you see
So greedy was he
He died for a single dinner;
And I hope that you
Will believe this true
And never be such a sinner.

COME ALL YE JOLLY SPORTSMEN

Come all ye jolly sportsmen,
Who like to chase a fox,
Who like to chase Beau Reynard
Among the hills and rocks.

Come-a-hooch, come-a-hooch, come-a-hi-lo,
Along the merry stream;
Away with a rowdy bow-wow-wow,
The bugle horn sings rack-u-liah,
As over the hills we run, dear boys,
Over the hills we run.

The first I saw was a maiden,
Combing out her locks;
She said she saw Beau Reynard
Among her geese and flocks.

The next I saw was a shepherd,
Watching o'er his flocks;
He said he saw Beau Reynard
Among the hills and rocks.

The next I saw was a school boy,
Coming from his school;
He said he saw Beau Reynard
While sitting on his stool.

The next I saw was a sportsman,
Cleaning out his gun;
He said he shot Beau Reynard
As in his den he run.

Come-a-hooch, come-a-hooch, come-a-hi-lo
Along the merry stream.
Away with a rowdy bow-wow-wow
The bugle horn sings rack-u-liah
As over the hills we run, dear boys,
Over the hills we run.

LITTLE FOX LOST

"It is dark in the world," wept the little fox,
"And I don't know where I am!
  There are three big sheep in that uphill field
  And a great big black-faced ram!"

"It is dark in the wood," said the little fox,
"And I've lost the starmoss way!
  The trees are tall and my fur is wet—
  What will my mother say?

"My fur is wet with the starlit dew,
  A cobweb tickles my nose,
  And my heart is a grasshopper wild in my chest—
  Where *am* I, do you suppose?"

"It is dark in the world!" sobbed the little fox.
"This path must be wrong! Here's another—"
"You're safe at my side! You're right at the door!
  Big foxes don't cry!" said his mother.

—Frances Frost

NIGHT OF WIND

How lost is the little fox at the borders of night,
Poised in the forest of fern, in the trample of wind!
Caught by the blowing cold of the mountain
     darkness,
He shivers and runs under tall trees, whimpering,
Brushing the tangles of dew. Pausing and
     running,
He searches the warm and shadowy hollow, the
     deep
Home on the mountain's side where the nuzzling,
     soft
Bodies of little foxes may hide and sleep.

—Frances Frost

THE SPUN GOLD FOX

Sing in the silver fog of night,
Voice of a foxhound, bellow-bright,
Sing me the silver song of fox,
Wary and watching the moon-dipped rocks.
Quivering nostril, lifted paw,
Sniffing the mist for the smell of dog.
Sing me foxhound, lemon-white,
Sing me the song of a fox tonight.
Bay me the story, old, old, old,
Of a fox that runs and a moon that's cold;
In the valley, the hill, near the speckled rocks,
Bay me the run of the spun gold fox.

—*Patricia Hubbell*

THE FALSE FOX

The false fox came unto our croft,
And so our geese full fast he sought.
With how, fox, how, with hey, fox, hey!
Come no more unto our house to bear our geese away!

The false fox came unto our sty,
And took our geese there by and by.

The false fox came into our yerd,
And there he made the geese aferd.

The false fox came unto our gate,
And took our geese there where they sate.

The false fox came to our hall door,
And shrove our geese there in the floor.

The false fox came into our hall,
And assoiled our geese both great and small.

The false fox came unto our coop,
And there he made our geese to stoop.

He took a goose fast by the neck,
And the goose thoo began to queck.

The goodwife came out in her smock,
And at the goose she threw her rok.

The goodman came out with his flail,
And smote the fox upon the tail.

He threw a goose upon his back,
And furth he went thoo with his pack.

The goodman swore if that he might,
He would him slee or it were night.

The false fox went into his den,
And there he was full merry then.

He came ayen yet the next week,
And took away both hen and cheke.

The goodman said unto his wife,
'This false fox liveth a merry life.'

The false fox came upon a day,
And with our geese he made affray.

He took a goose fast by the neck,
And made her to say 'wheccumquek.'

'I pray thee, fox', said the goose thoo,
'Take of my feders but not of my toe.'

THE FOX AND THE CHICKENS

The fox pursues the chicks.
He snares them with his tricks.
He calls them with his flute—
he'll eat them all, the brute!

Beware, O hens and cocks,
and never trust a fox!

—Christian Morgenstern